Dec.
2015

ERIN!

For the gourmet
cook in our family!

Love, Mom

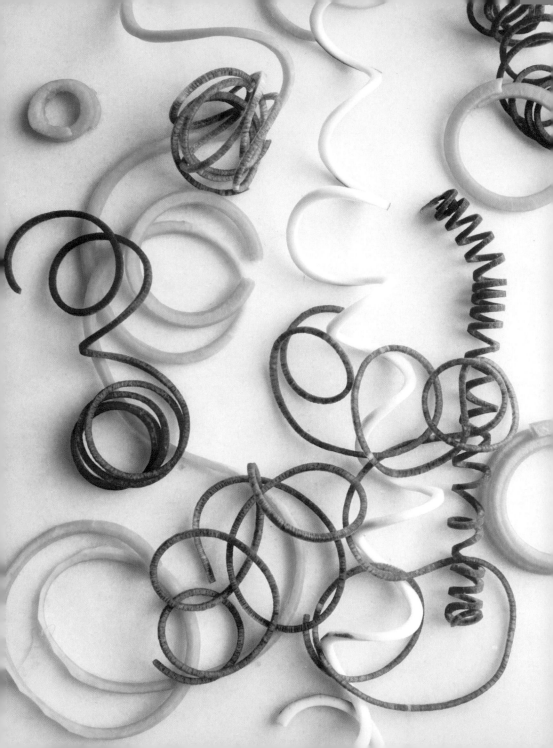

the spiralizer
COOKBOOK 2.0

DEVELOPED BY
WILLIAMS
SONOMA
TEST KITCHEN

Photographs Maren Caruso

weldon**owen**

contents

Welcome to Spiralizing 2.0

The Spiralizer is a versatile kitchen tool that will change the way you cook. In the Williams-Sonoma Test Kitchen, we use this innovative spiral slicer to create noodles, shoestrings, angel hair strands, and thin shreds or slices from a wide variety of fruits and vegetables. Not only does the Spiralizer offer a unique and often beautiful way to incorporate more fresh produce into meals, it's also an excellent tool for home cooks who want to eat a more plant-based diet. This quick and efficient machine wastes little to none of the produce and preps ingredients in a fraction of the time it takes using a knife or other cutting device.

The pages that follow include a primer showing step-by-step how easy it is to use the Spiralizer to prepare a wide variety of ingredients—from bell peppers to sweet potatoes. More than 20 recipes are featured, from breakfast to dinner, snacks to drinks. Start the day off right with Breakfast Hash with Crispy Sweet Potato Spirals (page 17) or Baked Eggs with Zucchini (page 13). The Mediterranean Quinoa Salad (page 20) and Shrimp Spring Rolls with Peanut Sauce (page 24) are both brimming with fresh spiralized vegetables and make a perfect weekday lunch. The Zucchini, Mushroom & Caramelized Onion Pizza (page 27) and Chicken Pho with Daikon Radish Noodles (page 32) are crowd-pleasing dinners that can be prepared in minutes. Impress guests with the Lemon–Olive Oil Upside-Down Cake (page 43) or Pear & Hazelnut Frangipane Tart (page 47). You'll find all of these creative dishes and more, including ideas for making the most of your Spiralizer from morning to night.

Spiralizer Blades

The Spiralizer comes with up to four blades, and each one creates a unique shape.

What can be spiralized?

A wide range of fruits and vegetables can be spiralized. For best results, the item should have a solid core or a firm outer layer.

- apples
- beets
- bell peppers
- broccoli stalks
- butternut squash
- cabbage
- carrots
- cucumbers
- daikon
- fennel
- jicama
- kohlrabi
- lemons
- onions
- parsnips
- pears
- potatoes
- radishes
- shallots
- zucchini
- and more!

A The Straight Blade

This versatile blade creates a wide ribbon shape, similar to pappardelle pasta. The blade is also used to shred cabbage; slice onions, shallots, and lemons; and shave produce into paper-thin slices for gratins, tarts, and chips.

B The Chipper Blade

This blade produces a thick, round, noodlelike shape. It is used to create thick vegetable strands for baked dishes and hearty salads.

C The Fine Shredder Blade

This blade makes thin, round noodles, akin to spaghetti. It works with a wide array of produce, which can be quickly sautéed for a pastalike dish or left uncooked for a refreshing raw salad. These thin spirals can also be baked into pancakes or cakes.

D The Angel Hair Shredder Blade

This thinner version of the Fine Shredder Blade creates strands similar to angel hair pasta. These ultrathin strands are perfect to use as a nonbulky stuffing for burritos and wraps or as delicate noodles in a broth.

The Straight Blade  **A**   **B** The Chipper Blade

The Fine Shredder Blade **C**   **D** The Angel Hair Shredder Blade

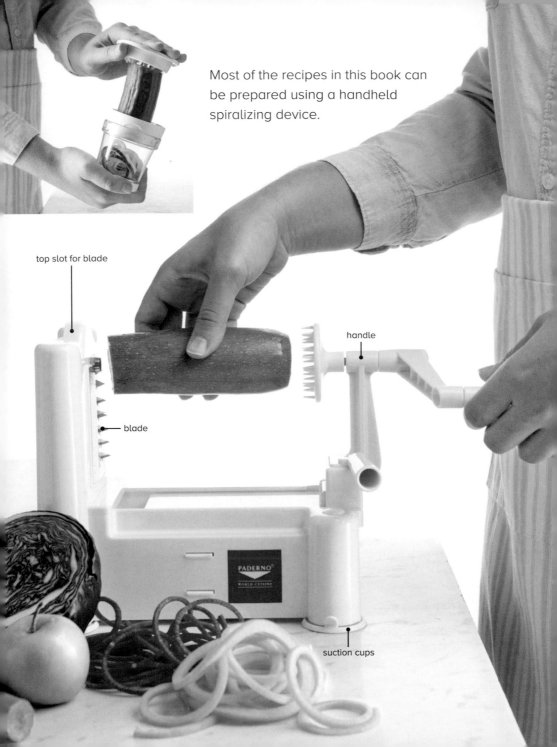

Most of the recipes in this book can be prepared using a handheld spiralizing device.

top slot for blade

handle

blade

PADERNO
WORLD CUISINE

suction cups

Spiralizing Primer

Working with the Spiralizer is a simple 6-step process. Consult the manufacturers' instructions to assemble the machine, then follow the steps below. Use caution handling the blades and the sharp-pointed handle.

1 Place the Spiralizer on a nonporous work surface, like a countertop or marble board. Push firmly on the suction cups to secure the machine to the surface.

2 Place your desired blade into the top slot. The extra blades are stored in the plastic drawers on the underside of the machine.

3 Prep your vegetables or fruit. Peel them, if necessary, then cut off both ends to create 2 straight, flat surfaces.

4 Align the vegetable or fruit so that the small cylindrical protrusion near the blade is positioned in the center. Once aligned, push the vegetable in firmly.

5 Holding the vegetable or fruit in one hand, use your other hand to slide the handle toward the vegetable. Push the teeth of the handle into the end of the vegetable until it holds securely.

6 Crank the handle, applying even pressure toward the blade. The spiralized vegetable or fruit will emerge from the other side of the machine; if desired, place a bowl on the other side of the Spiralizer to collect the food as it falls from the blade.

Baked Eggs with Zucchini

A great go-to brunch recipe, this easy and delicious dish can be served family style in a large baking dish or offered in individual servings in small ramekins. You can also use crumbled *cotija* cheese in place of the feta.

Preheat the oven to 375°F. Spiralize the onion and zucchini using the Fine Shredder Blade, stopping to cut the strands every 3–4 rotations.

In a large frying pan over medium heat, warm the oil. Add the onion and zucchini, and then season with salt and black pepper. Cook, stirring occasionally, until the onion is translucent and the zucchini is tender, about 5 minutes. Add the cayenne, paprika, thyme, and vinegar and cook, stirring occasionally, for 2 minutes. Add the tomatoes and their juices, reduce the heat to medium-low, and cook until slightly reduced, about 10 minutes. Adjust the seasoning with salt and black pepper.

Transfer the tomato sauce to a large baking dish or soufflé dish and crack the eggs into the sauce, spacing them evenly apart. Alternatively, divide the sauce among four 6-oz ramekins, crack an egg into the center of each, and place the ramekins on a baking sheet. Use a spoon to gently incorporate the egg whites into the tomato sauce, taking care not to break the yolks. Sprinkle each yolk with a small pinch of salt and a grinding of black pepper.

Bake until the yolks are set to your liking, 10–15 minutes. Top with the parsley and feta cheese and serve warm.

1 yellow onion, peeled and ends trimmed

2 zucchini, ends trimmed

1 tablespoon extra-virgin olive oil

Kosher salt and freshly ground black pepper

1 teaspoon cayenne pepper

1 teaspoon sweet paprika

1 tablespoon chopped fresh thyme

1 tablespoon sherry vinegar

1 can (28 oz) whole peeled tomatoes, roughly chopped, with juices

4 large eggs

¼ cup chopped fresh flat-leaf parsley

¼ cup crumbled feta cheese

SERVES 4

Apple Pancakes

Spiralized apples provide a fun decoration for these pancakes, but firm pears will also work in their place. Kids will love these for weekend breakfasts, especially when drizzled with warm maple syrup.

---

2 large eggs

2 cups all-purpose flour, sifted

⅓ cup granulated sugar

2 teaspoons baking powder

1 teaspoon baking soda

1 teaspoon kosher salt

2 teaspoons ground cinnamon

1 teaspoon ground ginger

½ teaspoon ground cloves

2¾ cups buttermilk

4 tablespoons unsalted butter, melted

2 teaspoons vanilla extract

2 Granny Smith apples, peeled and ends trimmed

Nonstick cooking spray

2 tablespoons firmly packed light brown sugar

SERVES 4

Preheat the oven to 200°F.

In a large bowl, whisk the eggs until frothy. Add the flour, the granulated sugar, baking powder, baking soda, salt, cinnamon, ginger, cloves, buttermilk, butter, and vanilla. Stir just until the batter is smooth and no lumps of flour remain; do not overmix.

Spiralize the apples using the Fine Shredder Blade, stopping to cut the strands every 3–4 rotations and arranging them in 8 small bunches.

Heat a griddle or nonstick frying pan over medium-high heat until a few drops of water flicked onto the surface skitter across it. Lightly coat the griddle with nonstick cooking spray.

For each pancake, sprinkle ½ teaspoon brown sugar on a small bunch of spiralized apples and place on the griddle. Using a ladle, add about ⅓ cup of the batter on top of the apples. Cook until bubbles form on top and the batter is set, about 2 minutes. Using a spatula, flip the pancakes and cook until golden brown on the other side, about 2 minutes longer. Transfer to a baking sheet and keep warm in the oven. Repeat to cook the remaining pancakes.

Breakfast Burritos

These hearty burritos are inspired by the breakfast comfort food served at many diners. Like their restaurant counterpart, these will keep you well satiated until lunchtime rolls around.

1 small red onion, peeled and ends trimmed

1 red bell pepper, stemmed and seeded

1 large russet potato, peeled and ends trimmed

4 tablespoons vegetable oil

Kosher salt and freshly ground pepper

8 large eggs

1 cup shredded Cheddar cheese

4 flour tortillas, each 10 inches in diameter, warmed

2 Roma tomatoes, diced

1 avocado, pitted, peeled, and diced

Hot-pepper sauce, for serving (optional)

SERVES 4

Spiralize the onion and bell pepper using the Straight Blade, stopping to cut the strands every 3–4 rotations. Transfer to a bowl. Set aside. Spiralize the potato using the Angel Hair Shredder Blade, stopping to cut the strands every 3–4 rotations. Transfer to another bowl and rinse with cold water until the water runs clear, then drain well.

In a large nonstick frying pan over medium-high heat, warm 1 tablespoon of the oil. Add the onion and bell pepper, season with salt and pepper, and cook, stirring occasionally, until tender, about 8 minutes. Return the onion mixture to the bowl. In the same pan over medium-high heat, warm 2 tablespoons of the oil. Add the potato, season with salt and pepper, and cook, stirring occasionally, until golden brown and tender, about 10 minutes. Transfer to a clean bowl.

In another bowl, whisk the eggs and season with salt and pepper. In the same pan over medium heat, warm the remaining 1 tablespoon oil. Add the eggs and cook, stirring occasionally, until large curds just start to form, about 1 minute. Add the cheese and cook, stirring frequently, until the cheese is melted and the eggs are softly scrambled but still moist, about 1 minute longer.

Put one-fourth of the scrambled eggs along the bottom third of each tortilla. Divide the onion mixture, potato, tomatoes, and avocado on top. Sprinkle with hot-pepper sauce, if using. Fold in the sides of each tortilla and roll up tightly around the filling. Serve right away.

Breakfast Hash with Crispy Sweet Potato Spirals

Crispy sweet potatoes and spicy Italian sausage are the stars in this unexpected take on a classic. To take this breakfast dish to the next level, top with a poached or fried egg.

Fill a wide, deep, heavy-bottomed pot or Dutch oven two-thirds full with canola oil and heat over medium-high heat to 350°F on a deep-frying thermometer. Line a plate with paper towels.

Meanwhile, spiralize the onion and sweet potato using the Chipper Blade, stopping to cut the strands every 3–4 rotations.

In a large frying pan over medium heat, warm the olive oil. Add the onion, half of the sweet potato, a pinch of salt, and a few grindings of black pepper. Cook, stirring frequently, until the onion and sweet potato are tender, about 10 minutes. Add the sausage and cook, stirring occasionally, until cooked through, about 5 minutes. Add the kale, red pepper flakes, lemon juice, and a pinch of salt. Cook, stirring occasionally, until the kale is wilted, about 2 minutes. Adjust the seasoning with salt and black pepper. Remove from the heat and cover to keep the hash warm.

Working in batches, deep-fry the remaining sweet potato, stirring occasionally with a skimmer or slotted spoon, until crispy, 4–6 minutes per batch. Using the skimmer, transfer the crispy sweet potato spirals to the paper towel–lined plate and immediately season with salt.

Transfer the hash to a serving dish and top with the crispy sweet potato spirals. Serve right away.

Canola oil, for frying

1 red onion, peeled and ends trimmed

1 sweet potato, peeled and ends trimmed

1 tablespoon extra-virgin olive oil

Kosher salt and freshly ground black pepper

¼ lb spicy Italian sausage, removed from casing and crumbled

1 bunch Tuscan kale, stemmed and leaves roughly chopped

1 teaspoon red pepper flakes

Juice of 1 lemon

SERVES 4

Apple-Cabbage Salad with Bacon & Candied Walnuts

Salty, sweet, and sour, this salad has plenty of crunch and eye appeal. A bit of bacon fat enriches the dressing. Serve alongside barbecued ribs or pulled pork sandwiches.

½ lb bacon, diced

1 cup walnut halves

2 tablespoons maple syrup

3 tablespoons cider vinegar

2 tablespoons whole-grain mustard

¼ cup vegetable oil

Kosher salt and freshly ground pepper

1 large green or red cabbage (about 2 lb), ends trimmed and outer leaves removed

1 small red onion, peeled and ends trimmed

2 carrots, peeled and ends trimmed

2 apples, such as Fuji or Gala, peeled and ends trimmed

SERVES 8–10

Line a plate with paper towels. In a large nonstick frying pan over medium-high heat, cook the bacon, stirring occasionally, until crisp, about 5 minutes. Transfer to the prepared plate. Pour the bacon fat into a small bowl and set aside. Wipe out the pan with paper towels.

Line a baking sheet with parchment paper. In the same pan over medium-high heat, combine the walnuts and maple syrup. Cook, stirring frequently, until the nuts are toasted and glazed, about 3 minutes. Transfer to the prepared baking sheet and let cool.

In a bowl, whisk together 2 tablespoons of the reserved bacon fat, the vinegar, mustard, oil, 2 teaspoons salt, and ½ teaspoon pepper to make a dressing. Set aside.

Cut a slit in one side of the cabbage and the onion, stopping near the center. Spiralize the cabbage and onion using the Straight Blade, stopping to cut the strands every 3–4 rotations, and transfer to a large bowl. Spiralize the carrots with the Chipper Blade and the apples with the Fine Shredder Blade, stopping to cut the strands every 3–4 rotations, and add to the bowl. Pour the dressing over the salad and toss thoroughly to coat. Add the bacon and walnuts and toss to combine. Adjust the seasoning with salt and pepper and serve.

Mediterranean Quinoa Salad

This riff on tabbouleh salad is chock-full of fresh vegetables and includes many of the same components as the classic version, but with a slightly more sophisticated look.

---

5 tablespoons extra-virgin olive oil

1 cup quinoa, rinsed well and drained

Kosher salt and freshly ground pepper

Finely grated zest and juice of 1 lemon

1 clove garlic, minced

1 shallot, finely diced

2 carrots, peeled and ends trimmed

1 English cucumber, ends trimmed

1½ cups cherry tomatoes, halved

¾ cup finely chopped fresh flat-leaf parsley

¾ cup crumbled feta cheese

SERVES 6–8

In a large saucepan over medium-high heat, warm 1 tablespoon of the oil. Add the quinoa and cook, stirring constantly, until lightly toasted, about 2 minutes. Add 1½ cups water and ½ teaspoon salt and bring to a boil. Reduce the heat to low, cover, and cook for 15 minutes. Remove from the heat and let stand, covered, for 5 minutes. Transfer to a bowl and fluff with a fork. Let cool.

Meanwhile, in a small bowl, whisk together the lemon zest, lemon juice, garlic, shallot, the remaining 4 tablespoons oil, ¾ teaspoon salt, and ¼ teaspoon pepper to make a vinaigrette. Set aside.

Spiralize the carrots and the cucumber using the Angel Hair Shredder Blade, stopping to cut the strands every 3–4 rotations. Transfer the carrot strands to a large bowl. Transfer the cucumber strands to a colander and toss with 1 teaspoon salt. Drain for 10 minutes, then transfer to the bowl with the carrots.

Add the quinoa, tomatoes, parsley, feta cheese, and vinaigrette and toss to combine.

Mexican Salad with Grilled Chicken

This crisp, refreshing main-course salad is just the thing for those warm-weather months. To round out the meal, serve tortilla chips and guacamole or your favorite salsa.

Prepare a medium-hot fire in a charcoal or gas grill or preheat a lightly oiled stove-top grill pan over medium-high heat.

In a small bowl, stir together the cumin, 1½ teaspoons salt, and ¼ teaspoon pepper. Sprinkle on both sides of the chicken. Place the chicken on the grill or pan and cook, turning once, until nicely grill-marked and cooked through, about 6 minutes per side. Transfer the chicken to a cutting board and cover loosely with aluminum foil.

In a large bowl, whisk together the lime juice, oil, cilantro, honey, and 1 teaspoon salt to make a vinaigrette. Cut a slit in one side of the onion, stopping near the center. Spiralize the onion using the Straight Blade, stopping to cut the strands every 3–4 rotations. Add the onion to the bowl with the vinaigrette and let stand for at least 10 minutes

Add the lettuce to the bowl. Cut a slit in one side of the jicama, stopping near the center. Spiralize the jicama using the Fine Shredder Blade, stopping to cut the strands every 3–4 rotations, and transfer to the bowl. Add the corn, beans, and tomatoes to the bowl and toss well. Season with salt and pepper.

Divide the salad among 6 bowls. Cut the chicken diagonally and fan out on top of each salad. Sprinkle the cheese on top. Serve right away.

5 tablespoons extra-virgin olive oil, plus more for stove-top grilling

½ teaspoon ground cumin

Kosher salt and freshly ground pepper

6 skinless, boneless chicken thighs (about 1½ lb total weight)

¼ cup fresh lime juice

¼ cup finely chopped fresh cilantro

2 teaspoons honey

1 small red onion, peeled and ends trimmed

½ small head iceberg lettuce, thinly sliced

1 jicama, peeled and ends trimmed

Kernels from 1 ear of corn (about 1 cup)

1 can (15 oz) black beans, rinsed and drained

1 cup cherry tomatoes, halved

½ cup crumbled *cotija* or feta cheese

SERVES 6

Sweet Potato & Zucchini Haystack

Strapped for time? Skip the homemade aioli and season 1 cup of store-bought mayonnaise with the lemon zest and chopped herbs for a speedy and equally delicious sauce.

To make the aioli, in a mini food processor, combine the garlic, egg, mustard, lemon zest, and lemon juice and pulse a few times to blend. With the motor running, add the olive oil in a slow, steady stream and process until the aioli is emulsified, stopping to scrape down the sides of the bowl as needed. Add the dill and parsley and pulse until combined. Season with salt and pepper. Store in an airtight container in the refrigerator for up to 1 week.

Fill a wide, deep, heavy-bottomed pot or Dutch oven two-thirds full with canola oil and heat over medium-high heat to 350°F on a deep-frying thermometer. Line a plate with paper towels.

Meanwhile, spiralize the russet potato, sweet potato, and zucchini using the Fine Shredder Blade, stopping to cut the strands every 3–4 rotations. Spread out the russet potato on a baking sheet and pat with paper towels to absorb excess moisture.

Working in batches, deep-fry the russet potato, stirring occasionally with a skimmer or slotted spoon, until crispy and golden brown, 4–6 minutes per batch. Using the skimmer, transfer the fries to the prepared plate and season with salt. Repeat to fry the sweet potato and zucchini. Stack the potatoes and zucchini on a serving platter. Serve right away with the aioli.

For the aioli

1 clove garlic

1 large egg

1 teaspoon Dijon mustard

Zest and juice of 1 lemon

½ cup extra-virgin olive oil

2 tablespoons
fresh dill leaves

2 tablespoons fresh
flat-leaf parsley leaves

Kosher salt and freshly
ground pepper

Canola oil, for frying

1 russet potato, peeled
and ends trimmed

1 sweet potato, peeled
and ends trimmed

1 zucchini, ends trimmed

Kosher salt

SERVES 4

Shrimp Spring Rolls with Peanut Sauce

Mix and match a variety of brightly colored vegetables in this eye-catching appetizer. Be sure to use a candy cane beet (also known as Chioggia); a red one will bleed onto the other ingredients.

---

1 English cucumber, ends trimmed

1 carrot, peeled and ends trimmed

2 watermelon radishes, peeled and ends trimmed

1 candy cane (Chioggia) beet, peeled and ends trimmed

8 large cooked shrimp, peeled and deveined

Juice of 1 lemon

1 tablespoon toasted sesame oil

1 avocado, pitted, peeled, and thinly sliced

8–16 rice paper wrappers

½ cup smooth peanut butter

Juice of 1 lime

1 tablespoon soy sauce

1 tablespoon firmly packed light brown sugar

Black sesame seeds and sprouts, for garnish

SERVES 8

Spiralize the cucumber, carrot, radishes, and beet using the Angel Hair Shredder Blade, stopping to cut the strands every 3–4 rotations. Transfer the vegetables to a large bowl. Add the shrimp, lemon juice, and sesame oil and stir to combine.

Fill a large bowl with hot water. Soak 1 rice paper wrapper until soft, about 1 minute, then place on a clean work surface. Place a spoonful of the shrimp mixture in the center of the wrapper. Add 1–2 slices avocado. Fold the ends in over the filling and roll up tightly from the edge closest to you. If the spring roll is not secure, roll it inside of a second wrapper. Repeat with the remaining wrappers and filling.

In a bowl, stir together the peanut butter, lime juice, soy sauce, and brown sugar until smooth. Add water to thin the sauce to the desired consistency. Transfer to a small serving bowl. The sauce can be stored in an airtight container in the refrigerator for up to 1 day.

Arrange the spring rolls on a platter and garnish with sesame seeds and sprouts. Serve the peanut dipping sauce alongside.

Zucchini, Mushroom & Caramelized Onion Pizza

Caramelized onions and a duo of cheeses provide a deeply flavored base for this sauceless pizza. No baking stone? No problem: use an inverted baking sheet instead.

Place a baking stone on a rack in the lower third of the oven. Preheat to 500°F.

Cut a slit in one side of each onion, stopping near the center. Spiralize the onions using the Straight Blade. In a large sauté pan over medium-high heat, warm 2 tablespoons of the oil. Add the onions and cook, stirring occasionally, until browned, about 15 minutes. Add the garlic and thyme, season with salt and pepper, and cook, stirring, until fragrant, about 1 minute. Transfer to a bowl. In the same pan over medium-high heat, warm 1 tablespoon of the oil. Add the mushrooms, season with salt and pepper, and cook, stirring occasionally, until browned, about 6 minutes. Transfer to another bowl.

Spiralize the bell pepper using the Straight Blade, stopping to cut the strands every 3–4 rotations. Transfer to another bowl and toss with salt and pepper. Spiralize the zucchini using the Fine Shredder Blade, stopping to cut the strands every 3–4 rotations. Transfer to another bowl and toss with salt, pepper, and the remaining 1 tablespoon oil.

Transfer the doughs to a lightly floured pizza peel. Divide the onions, cheese, mushrooms, bell pepper, and zucchini among the pizzas. Slide one onto the baking stone. Bake until the crust is crisp and the cheese is bubbly, about 10 minutes. Using the peel, transfer the pizza to a cutting board. Slice, garnish with basil, and serve right away. Repeat to bake the remaining pizza.

2 yellow onions, peeled and ends trimmed

4 tablespoons olive oil

1 teaspoon minced garlic

1 teaspoon chopped fresh thyme

Kosher salt and freshly ground pepper

½ lb cremini mushrooms, brushed clean and sliced

1 red bell pepper, stemmed and seeded

2 zucchini, ends trimmed

All-purpose flour, for dusting

1 cup *each* shredded Gruyère cheese and mozzarella cheese, stirred together

1 lb homemade or store-bought pizza dough, halved, and stretched into two 10-inch rounds

Fresh basil leaves, for garnish

MAKES TWO
10-INCH PIZZAS

Thai Cucumber Salad with Flank Steak

Spiralizing cucumbers creates an elegant-looking salad. Served with sliced flank steak and a sweet-and-salty, Thai-style vinaigrette, this is a delicious meal that's fit for company.

¼ cup fresh lime juice

2 tablespoons rice wine vinegar

2 tablespoons fish sauce

2 tablespoons firmly packed light brown sugar

2 cloves garlic, minced

3 tablespoons canola oil

1 teaspoon toasted sesame oil

Kosher salt

1 lb flank steak

2 English cucumbers, ends trimmed

¼ cup fresh mint leaves, julienned

¼ cup roasted peanuts, chopped

½ red onion, thinly sliced

SERVES 4

In a small bowl, whisk together the lime juice, vinegar, fish sauce, brown sugar, garlic, canola oil, sesame oil, and a large pinch of salt to make a vinaigrette. Place the flank steak in a large baking dish and pour half of the vinaigrette over the steak. Cover and refrigerate for at least 1 hour or up to 12 hours. Store the remaining vinaigrette in an airtight container in the refrigerator until ready to use.

Prepare a medium-hot fire in a charcoal or gas grill, or preheat a stove-top grill pan over medium-high heat. Place the steak on the grill or pan and cook, turning once, for 9–11 minutes total for medium-rare. Transfer the steak to a cutting board, cover loosely with aluminum foil, and let rest for 5–10 minutes.

Meanwhile, spiralize the cucumbers using the Straight Blade, stopping to cut the strands every 3–4 rotations. Transfer to a bowl and toss with the reserved vinaigrette. Top with the mint, peanuts, onion, and a large pinch of salt.

Thinly slice the steak across the grain, reserving any accumulated juices, and serve with the cucumber salad. Drizzle the meat juices over the top.

Mason Jar Salad

In this on-the-go salad, sturdy vegetables are layered over the dressing, so the remaining ingredients stay crisp until you're ready to eat. Feel free to swap in other vegetables, grains, and nuts. Add chickpeas, hard-boiled eggs, or cooked chicken for more protein.

Spiralize the carrot, radishes, and cucumber using the Fine Shredder Blade, stopping to cut the strands every 3–4 rotations.

In a small bowl, whisk together the oil and lemon juice to make a vinaigrette. Season with salt and pepper. Pour the vinaigrette into a wide-mouthed mason jar. Layer the quinoa on top of the dressing. Place the carrot, radishes, cucumber, and tomatoes on top of the quinoa. Layer the remaining ingredients in this order: cheese, avocado, and almonds (if using). Place the salad greens on top and screw the lid on the jar. Refrigerate until ready to eat, up to 2 days.

To serve, shake the jar to distribute the vinaigrette and eat right out of the jar or transfer to a bowl.

½ **carrot, peeled and end trimmed**

2 radishes, peeled and ends trimmed

½ **English cucumber, end trimmed**

2 tablespoons extra-virgin olive oil

1 tablespoon fresh lemon juice

Kosher salt and freshly ground pepper

½ **cup cooked quinoa or brown rice**

¼ **cup cherry tomatoes, halved**

1 oz feta cheese, crumbled

½ **avocado, pitted, peeled, and thinly sliced**

2 tablespoons toasted almonds or sunflower seeds (optional)

½ **cup salad greens**

SERVES 1

Chicken Pho with Daikon Radish Noodles

Fresh and hearty, this faux pho can be transformed into a delicious vegetarian soup by using vegetable broth and tofu instead of chicken. If you can't find daikon radish, spiralize a zucchini instead.

1 yellow onion, peeled and ends trimmed

1 lb daikon radish, peeled and ends trimmed

2 tablespoons extra-virgin olive oil

2 cloves garlic, minced

½ lb shiitake mushrooms, brushed clean, stemmed, and thinly sliced

1 teaspoon ground cinnamon

1 teaspoon red pepper flakes

6 cups chicken broth

2 skin-on, bone-in chicken breast halves (about 1½ lb total weight)

½-inch piece peeled fresh ginger, sliced into thin rounds

Kosher salt

2 teaspoons soy sauce

Sliced green onions, sliced jalapeño chile, fresh cilantro or mint leaves, white sesame seeds, and/ or lime wedges, for serving

SERVES 4

Spiralize the onion using the Fine Shredder Blade, stopping to cut the strands every 3–4 rotations. Spiralize the daikon radish using the Angel Hair Shredder Blade. Use scissors to cut the daikon spirals into noodle-length pieces. Set aside.

In a large pot over medium-high heat, warm the oil. Add the onion and cook, stirring occasionally, until soft and translucent, about 4 minutes. Add the garlic and mushrooms and cook, stirring occasionally, until the mushrooms are tender, about 3 minutes. Add the cinnamon and red pepper flakes and cook for 1 minute. Add the broth, chicken, ginger, and a pinch of salt. Bring to a boil, then reduce the heat to medium-low and simmer until the chicken is cooked through, 20–25 minutes.

Using tongs, transfer the chicken to a plate. When cool enough to handle, remove the meat, discarding the skin and bones. Using a fork, shred the meat into bite-sized pieces.

Add the chicken, soy sauce, and daikon radish to the broth and stir to combine. Serve right away with green onion, jalapeño, cilantro or mint, sesame seeds, and/or lime wedges alongside.

Halibut & Summer Vegetables in Parchment

For a showstopper at your next dinner party, serve guests their own parchment pouch filled with fresh, lemony halibut and vegetables. Let them open it at the table and savor the wonderful aroma.

2 zucchini, ends trimmed

1 lemon, ends trimmed, plus juice of 1 lemon

2 cups cherry tomatoes, halved

Kosher salt and freshly ground pepper

4 halibut fillets, 6–8 oz each

¼ cup pine nuts, toasted

Extra-virgin olive oil, for drizzling

¼ cup fresh basil leaves, for garnish

SERVES 4

Preheat the oven to 400°F.

Spiralize the zucchini using the Fine Shredder Blade, stopping to cut the strands every 3–4 rotations. Spiralize the lemon using the Straight Blade.

In a bowl, toss together the zucchini, tomatoes, and lemon juice and season with salt and pepper. Sprinkle both sides of each halibut fillet with a pinch of salt and a grinding of pepper.

Cut 4 sheets of parchment paper, each 12 by 16 inches, and lay them on a work surface. Bring the short sides of each sheet together, fold the sheet in half, and crease, then open it flat. For each packet, spoon one-fourth of the zucchini mixture on one side of the crease and top with a halibut fillet. Place a few lemon spirals and one-fourth of the pine nuts on the fish, then drizzle lightly with oil.

Bring the uncovered side of the parchment over the fish and, starting at one end of the crease, fold the edges together to create a sealed packet. Place the packets on a baking sheet. Roast until the fish is just cooked through, 10–12 minutes. Carefully open the packets, garnish with basil, and serve warm. Alternatively, allow guests to open their own packets and pass the basil at the table.

Fresh Parsnip Pasta Primavera

Parnisps look so similar to pasta, you'll hardly be able to tell the difference. Here, reduced white wine and just a bit of butter and cream form a silky, yet light sauce.

Bring a large pot of water to a boil over high heat. Add the snap peas and cook until they turn bright green, 1–2 minutes. Using a slotted spoon, transfer the snap peas to a bowl of ice water. Drain and cut in half diagonally. Set aside.

Spiralize the parsnips using the Fine Shredder Blade, stopping to cut the strands every 3–4 rotations. Add the parsnips to the boiling water and cook until al dente (tender but firm to the bite), about 2 minutes. Drain and set aside.

In a large sauté pan over medium high heat, warm 2 tablespoons of the oil. Add the tomatoes and cook, stirring occasionally, until they are blistered and beginning to wilt, about 5 minutes. Transfer to a bowl.

In the same pan over medium heat, warm the remaining 1 tablespoon oil. Add the shallot, garlic, and red pepper flakes and cook, stirring occasionally, until the shallot is translucent, about 2 minutes. Add the wine and simmer until reduced by half, 1–2 minutes. Add the butter and cream and simmer until slightly reduced, 1–2 minutes.

Add the snap peas, tomatoes, and frozen peas and cook until the vegetables are warmed through, 1–2 minutes. Add the parsnips, lemon juice, and cheese and toss to combine. Add the herbs and toss again. Season to taste with salt. Serve right away, passing additional cheese at the table.

¼ lb sugar snap peas, trimmed

1 lb parsnips, peeled and ends trimmed

3 tablespoons olive oil

2 cups cherry tomatoes

1 shallot, chopped

2 cloves garlic, chopped

Pinch of red pepper flakes

½ cup white wine

2 tablespoons unsalted butter

¼ cup heavy cream

½ cup frozen peas

1 tablespoon fresh lemon juice

¼ cup grated *pecorino romano* cheese, plus more for serving

¼ cup chopped mixed fresh herbs, such as mint, chives, chervil, and flat-leaf parsley

Kosher salt

SERVES 4

Chicken Potpie

Spiralized vegetables and a lattice crust made from puff pastry lend a unique twist to classic potpie. If you'd like, bake the pastry trimmings and pass them at the table.

1 small yellow onion, peeled and ends trimmed

1 russet potato, peeled and ends trimmed

2 carrots, peeled and ends trimmed

½ cup unsalted butter

½ cup plus 1 tablespoon all-purpose flour, plus more for dusting

¼ cup white wine

3½ cups chicken broth

2 ribs celery, sliced

¼ lb button mushrooms, brushed clean and thinly sliced

1 tablespoon chopped fresh thyme

1 teaspoon chopped fresh tarragon

1 bay leaf

2 lb cubed cooked chicken

½ lb frozen peas

Kosher salt and freshly ground pepper

1 package (1 lb) frozen puff pastry, thawed

SERVES 6

Preheat the oven to 375°F.

Cut a slit in one side of the onion and in the potato, stopping near the center. Spiralize the onion and the potato using the Straight Blade. Spiralize the carrots using the Fine Shredder Blade, stopping to cut the strands every 3–4 rotations. Set aside.

In a large sauté pan over medium heat, melt the butter. Add the flour and cook, stirring constantly, until fragrant, about 2 minutes. Whisk in the wine. Slowly add the broth, whisking until smooth, and bring to a simmer. Add the onion, potato, carrots, celery, mushrooms, thyme, tarragon, and bay leaf and cook until the vegetables are almost tender, about 10 minutes. Add the chicken and peas and season with salt and pepper. Cook until just heated through, about 5 minutes longer. Let the filling cool for 20 minutes.

Meanwhile, on a lightly floured surface, gently unfold the puff pastry and cut into strips about 1 inch wide. Pour the filling into a 2-quart soufflé dish or deep baking dish. Arrange the puff pastry strips in a lattice pattern over the filling. Place the dish on a baking sheet. Bake until the pastry is golden brown and puffed, 15–20 minutes. Let cool for 10 minutes before serving.

Curly Fries with Fresh Herbs

We've put a fresh spin on classic French fries by spiralizing the potatoes. To help prevent spattering, be sure to dry the potatoes well before frying them in the hot oil.

Preheat the oven to 200°F.

Spiralize the potatoes using the Chipper Blade, stopping to cut the strands every 3–4 rotations.

Rinse the potatoes in cold water until the water runs clear, then drain in a colander. Place a handful of the potatoes at a time in a kitchen towel and press firmly to absorb the water.

Fill a wide, deep, heavy-bottomed pot or Dutch oven two-thirds full with canola oil and heat over medium-high heat to 350°F on a deep-frying thermometer. Line a baking sheet with paper towels. Place a wire cooling rack on another baking sheet.

Working in batches, fry the potatoes, stirring occasionally with a skimmer or slotted spoon, until golden and crispy, 2–3 minutes per batch. Using the skimmer, transfer the fries to the paper towel–lined baking sheet and immediately season with salt. When drained, transfer the fries to the rack-lined baking sheet and keep warm in the oven until ready to serve.

To serve, transfer the fries to a large bowl, garnish with herbs, and season with pepper. Serve right away.

2 lb russet potatoes, peeled and ends trimmed

Canola or vegetable oil, for frying

Kosher salt and freshly ground pepper

Fresh herbs, such as parsley, cilantro, or rosemary, for garnish

SERVES 4

Butternut Squash & Bacon Tart

Topped with bacon, dotted with tart goat cheese, and sprinkled with crispy sage leaves, this pretty winter squash tart is fit for entertaining or delicious for breakfast, dinner, or an anytime snack.

For the pastry

1 large egg yolk

2 tablespoons ice water

1¼ cups all-purpose flour, plus more for dusting

¼ teaspoon kosher salt

½ cup cold unsalted butter, cut into small cubes

For the filling

1 butternut squash, about 3 lb, peeled and halved crosswise, seeded half reserved for another use

¼ lb bacon, chopped

1 clove garlic, minced

1 shallot, minced

Kosher salt and freshly ground pepper

2 oz goat cheese, crumbled

2 large eggs whisked with ½ cup heavy cream

3 or 4 fresh sage leaves

SERVES 8

To make the pastry, in a small bowl, whisk together the egg yolk and water. Set aside. In the bowl of a stand mixer fitted with the paddle, stir together the flour and salt. Add the butter and beat on medium-low speed until the texture resembles coarse cornmeal, with butter pieces no larger than small peas. Add the egg mixture and beat just until the dough pulls together. Shape into a disk, wrap well in plastic wrap, and refrigerate for at least 30 minutes or up to 2 days.

Preheat the oven to 375°F. On a lightly floured surface, roll out the dough into an 11-inch round or rectangle about ¼ inch thick. Transfer to a 9-inch round or 10-inch rectangular tart pan with a removable bottom. Fit the dough into the pan and trim the edges. Line the shell with aluminum foil and fill with pie weights. Bake until golden brown, about 15 minutes. Let cool completely on a wire rack. Remove the foil and pie weights.

Meanwhile, to make the filling, spiralize the squash using the Fine Shredder Blade, stopping to cut the strands every 3–4 rotations. Set aside. In a large sauté pan over medium-high heat, cook the bacon, stirring occasionally, until crispy, about 5 minutes. Add the garlic and shallot and cook, stirring, for 30 seconds. Add the squash and season with salt and pepper. Cook, stirring occasionally, until soft, 4–6 minutes. Transfer the squash mixture to the cooled tart shell. Sprinkle with the cheese.

Pour the egg-cream mixture evenly over the tart. Place the sage leaves on top. Bake until the tart is set and the sage leaves are crispy, 20–25 minutes. Let stand for 5 minutes before serving.

Lemon–Olive Oil Upside-Down Cake

Perfect for a dinner party or afternoon tea, this surprisingly light olive-oil cake topped with gorgeous lemon spirals is sure to be a winner on your dessert table. Try a candied lemon peel garnish for an elegant finish.

Preheat the oven to 350°F. Lightly butter a 9-inch springform pan. Line the bottom with a round of parchment paper, then butter or spray the parchment. Dust the bottom and sides of the pan with flour. Spiralize the 3 lemons using the Straight Blade. Fill a small saucepan with water and bring to a boil over high heat. Add the lemon slices and blanch for 15 seconds. Drain and place on a wire rack or kitchen towel to cool.

In a small saucepan over medium-high heat, combine the butter and brown sugar and heat, stirring occasionally, until the butter melts and the mixture begins to boil, about 3–4 minutes. Pour into the prepared pan. Let cool for 5 minutes, then arrange the lemon slices in a spiral, starting from the outside and working toward the center.

In a large bowl, combine the lemon zest and granulated sugar and gently rub with your fingertips to evenly distribute the zest. Add the milk, lemon juice, eggs, and oil and stir to combine. In another bowl, whisk together the flour, baking powder, baking soda, and ½ teaspoon salt. Add the flour mixture to the sugar mixture and whisk until well combined and smooth. Pour the batter over the lemon slices. Tap the pan gently on the counter to evenly distribute the batter and eliminate any air pockets. Bake until a toothpick inserted into the center of the cake comes out clean, 40–50 minutes. Let the cake cool completely in the pan on a wire rack. Remove the pan sides, invert the cake onto a serving platter, and peel off the parchment.

½ cup unsalted butter, plus more for greasing

1¾ cups all-purpose flour, plus more for dusting

3 lemons, ends trimmed, plus zest and juice of 2 lemons

½ cup firmly packed light brown sugar

1¼ cups granulated sugar

½ cup whole milk

3 large eggs

⅔ cup extra-virgin olive oil

1½ teaspoons baking powder

½ teaspoon baking soda

Kosher salt

SERVES 8–10

Apple Galette

Easy to throw together, this rustic tart makes a beautiful presentation.
Serve warm with a scoop of vanilla ice cream or a dollop of crème fraîche.

For the pastry

1¼ cups all-purpose flour,
plus more for dusting

1 tablespoon
granulated sugar

Kosher salt

½ cup cold unsalted butter,
cut into small cubes

3 tablespoons ice
water, or as needed

For the filling

2 firm apples, peeled
and ends trimmed

Juice of 1 lemon

3 tablespoons
granulated sugar

1–2 tablespoons
turbinado sugar, or
as needed (optional)

1 large egg yolk beaten
with 1 tablespoon
heavy cream (optional)

SERVES 6

To make the pastry, in a food processor, combine the flour, granulated sugar, and ½ teaspoon salt and pulse until well mixed. Add the butter and pulse until the mixture resembles coarse cornmeal, 8–10 seconds. Slowly add the ice water, 1 tablespoon at a time, and pulse just until the dough comes together. Shape into a disk, wrap well in plastic wrap, and refrigerate for at least 30 minutes or up to 2 days. Preheat the oven to 400°F.

To make the filling, spiralize the apples using the Fine Shredder Blade, stopping to cut the strands every 3–4 rotations. Transfer to a bowl and stir in the lemon juice and 2 tablespoons of the granulated sugar. Drain in a colander for 20 minutes. Stir in the remaining 1 tablespoon granulated sugar.

Cut a sheet of parchment paper the size of a baking sheet and dust with flour. Working directly on the parchment, roll out the dough into a 12-inch round about ⅛ inch thick. Trim the edges to form a neat round or leave untrimmed for a rustic look. Transfer the parchment and dough onto a baking sheet.

Arrange the apples evenly over the dough, leaving an uncovered border of 1–1½ inches. Sprinkle the dough with turbinado sugar, if using. Carefully fold the edges of the dough up and over the apples, loosely pleating the edges and leaving the center open. Brush the pastry with the egg yolk mixture, if using. Sprinkle turbinado sugar, if using, generously over the pastry.

Bake until the crust is golden brown and the juices are slightly bubbling, about 30 minutes. Let cool slightly before serving.

Pear & Hazelnut Frangipane Tart

For a beautiful garnish, sprinkle 2 tablespoons chopped toasted hazelnuts over the tart and dust with confectioners' sugar. You'll have enough frangipane for 2 tarts; refrigerate the rest for up to 1 week. The pastry crust can be made in advance and frozen for up to 2 months.

To make the pastry, split the vanilla bean and scrape the seeds using the back of a paring knife. In a food processor, pulse the flour, confectioners' sugar, salt, and vanilla bean seeds until well mixed. Add the butter and process until the mixture is coarse. Scrape down the bowl, add half of the egg, and pulse just until the dough comes together. Shape into a disk, wrap in plastic wrap, and refrigerate for at least 30 minutes.

Preheat the oven to 400°F. On a lightly floured surface, roll out the dough into an 11-inch round about ⅛ inch thick. Transfer to a 9-inch fluted tart pan with a removable bottom. Fit the dough into the pan and trim the edges. Freeze for 10 minutes. Place the pan on a baking sheet. Line the shell with foil and fill with pie weights. Bake until the edges are dry and set, 15–20 minutes. Carefully remove the foil and weights. Bake until the pastry is pale gold, 5–6 minutes longer. Let cool. Lower the oven to 350°F. Place the pears in a bowl and stir in the lemon juice and granulated sugar. Drain in a colander for 20 minutes.

To make the frangipane, skin the hazelnuts. In a food processor, pulse the nuts and confectioners' sugar until coarsely ground. Add the butter and pulse until creamy. Add the egg, extracts, and salt and pulse until well combined. Add the flour and pulse until incorporated. Spread half of the frangipane in the cooled tart shell. Arrange the pear slices in a spiral, starting from the outside. Bake until the pears are tender, about 20 minutes. Serve warm or let cool completely.

For the pastry

½ vanilla bean

1¼ cups all-purpose flour

¼ cup confectioners' sugar

½ teaspoon kosher salt

½ cup cold unsalted butter, cut into small cubes

1 large egg, lightly beaten

3 firm pears, spiralized using the Straight Blade

1 tablespoon fresh lemon juice

2 tablespoons granulated sugar

For the frangipane

¾ cup toasted hazelnuts

⅓ cup confectioners' sugar

6 tablespoons unsalted butter, at room temperature

1 large egg, lightly beaten

1 teaspoon vanilla extract

¼ teaspoon almond extract

Pinch of kosher salt

1 tablespoon all-purpose flour

SERVES 8–10

Chocolate Zucchini Quick Bread with Ganache

No one will ever guess that there's a zucchini in this delicious dessert, which gets a double hit of chocolate. Semisweet chocolate chips are baked into the bread and also melted into the ganache.

Nonstick cooking spray

1 zucchini, ends trimmed

⅔ cup firmly packed light brown sugar

⅓ cup canola oil

⅓ cup Greek yogurt

2 large eggs

1 teaspoon vanilla extract

1½ cups all-purpose flour

1 teaspoon ground cinnamon

½ teaspoon baking powder

½ teaspoon baking soda

Kosher salt

½ cup chopped pecans

1½ cups semisweet chocolate chips

½ cup heavy cream

SERVES 8–10

Preheat the oven to 350°F. Coat a 9-by-5-inch loaf pan with nonstick cooking spray.

Spiralize the zucchini using the Angel Hair Shredder Blade, then coarsely chop. Transfer to a large bowl. Add the brown sugar, oil, yogurt, eggs, and vanilla and stir until well combined.

In a bowl, stir together the flour, cinnamon, baking powder, baking soda, and a pinch of salt. Stir the flour mixture into the zucchini mixture until just combined. Fold in the pecans and ½ cup of the chocolate chips. Pour the batter into the prepared pan.

Bake until a toothpick inserted into the center of the bread comes out clean, 45–50 minutes. Let cool on a wire rack.

Just before serving, put the remaining 1 cup chocolate chips in a heatproof bowl. In a small saucepan over medium heat, bring the cream just to a simmer, 2–3 minutes. Pour the cream over the chocolate chips. Stir until the chocolate chips have melted and the mixture is smooth. Pour over the cooled bread and serve right away.

Cucumber Gimlet

Spiralized fruits and vegetables are not just for eating—they also work great in cocktails, mocktails, and spa water. This updated take on a cucumber gimlet shows off the versatility of the Spiralizer.

Make the simple syrup. Spiralize the cucumber using the Straight Blade.

In a cocktail shaker, muddle half of the cucumber and the gin. Let stand for 5 minutes. Add the lime juice, simple syrup, and ice cubes and shake well. Top with soda, if using. Pour into cocktail glasses and garnish with additional cucumber slices.

Simple Syrup

In a saucepan, combine equal parts sugar and water and stir to dissolve the sugar. Bring to a boil over high heat. Remove from the heat and let cool to room temperature. Store in an airtight container in the refrigerator for up to 1 month.

1 English cucumber, peeled and end trimmed

½ cup gin

2 tablespoons fresh lime juice

3 tablespoons simple syrup (see recipe)

Ice cubes

Dash of club soda (optional)

MAKES 2 COCKTAILS

Spiralized Spa Waters

It's easy to make fruit-flavored spa water at home, and these drinks look especially beautiful with spiralized fruit. Try the combinations here or create your own refreshing variations.

Apple-Lemon

1 Granny Smith apple, ends trimmed

1 lemon, ends trimmed

Still or sparkling water, for serving

Ice cubes, for serving

Cucumber-Strawberry-Basil

½ cucumber, end trimmed

3 or 4 fresh strawberries, hulled and sliced

4 fresh basil leaves

Still or sparkling water, for serving

Ice cubes, for serving

Lemon-Mint

1 lemon, ends trimmed

8 fresh mint leaves

Still or sparkling water, for serving

Ice cubes, for serving

SERVES 4

Apple-Lemon Spa Water

Spiralize the apple using the Fine Shredder Blade, stopping to cut the strands every 3–4 rotations. Spiralize the lemon using the Straight Blade, stopping to cut the strands every 3–4 rotations. Put the apple and lemon in a large pitcher or divide among 4 glasses. Add water and ice and serve.

Cucumber-Strawberry-Basil Spa Water

Spiralize the cucumber using the Straight Blade, stopping to cut the strands every 3–4 rotations. Put the cucumber, strawberries, and basil in a large pitcher or among between 4 glasses. Add water and ice and serve.

Lemon-Mint Spa Water

Spiralize the lemon using the Straight Blade, stopping to cut the strands every 3–4 rotations. Put the lemon and mint in a large pitcher or divide among 4 glasses. Add water and ice and serve.

Index

THE SPIRALIZER COOKBOOK 2.0

Conceived and produced by Weldon Owen, Inc.
In collaboration with Williams-Sonoma, Inc.
3250 Van Ness Avenue, San Francisco, CA 94109

A WELDON OWEN PRODUCTION
1045 Sansome Street, Suite 100
San Francisco, CA 94111
www.weldonowen.com

Copyright © 2015 Weldon Owen, Inc.
and Williams-Sonoma, Inc.
All rights reserved, including the right of
reproduction in whole or in part in any form.

Printed in the United States by Worzalla

First printed in 2015
10 9 8 7 6 5 4 3 2 1

Library of Congress Cataloging-in-Publication
data is available.

ISBN 13: 978-1-68188-026-6
ISBN 10: 1-68188-026-1

WELDON OWEN, INC.
President & Publisher Roger Shaw
SVP, Sales & Marketing Amy Kaneko
Finance Manager Philip Paulick

Associate Publisher Amy Marr
Associate Editor Emma Rudolph

Creative Director Kelly Booth
Art Director Marisa Kwek
Associate Art Director Lisa Berman

Production Director Chris Hemesath
Associate Production Director Michelle Duggan
Production Manager Michelle Woo

Photographer Maren Caruso
Food Stylist Lillian Kang
Prop Stylist Laura Cook

Weldon Owen is a division of **BONNIER**

ACKNOWLEDGMENTS

Weldon Owen wishes to thank the following people for their
generous support in producing this book: Amanda Anselmino,
Kris Balloun, Sean Franzen, Gloria Geller, Kim Laidlaw, and Elizabeth Parson.